The Predicament of Or

Shani Mootoo

Polestar Book Publishers
Vancouver

Copyright © 2001 by Shani Mootoo

All rights reserved. No part of this publication may be reproduced or transmitted in any form or by any means, electronic or mechanical, including photocopying, recording or by any information storage and retrieval system now known or to be invented, without permission in writing from the publisher.

Polestar Books and Raincoast Books gratefully acknowledge the support of the Government of Canada through the Book Publishing Industry Development Program, the Canada Council and the Department of Canadian Heritage. We also acknowledge the assistance of the Province of British Columbia through the British Columbia Arts Council.

Edited by Lynn Henry
Design by Val Speidel
Cover photograph © Masatoshi Makio/Photonica

National Library of Canada Cataloguing in Publication Data

Mootoo, Shani, 1957–
  The predicament of or

  Poems.
  ISBN 1-55192-416-1

  I. Title.
  PS8576.O622P73 2001   C811'.54   C2001-910222-4
  PR9199.3.M6353P73 2001

Polestar, an Imprint of Raincoast Books
9050 Shaughnessy Street
Vancouver, British Columbia
Canada   V6P 6E5

1 2 3 4 5 6 7 8 9 10

The Predicament of Or

THE GRIFFIN TRUST
For Excellence In Poetry

CANADIAN
2001
www.griffinpoetryprize.com

For Kathy

Contents

I

The Way You Bounce Off a Pane of Glass

Beach Composition I   11
Beach Composition II   12
Beach Composition III 13
A Talent for Breathing 18
Glass and Lace Wrought Iron   20
The Hole in the Hedge   23
Faith   26
Ceremonial   27
Exchanges   28
Poui's Hero   32
Hand-Held   34
Manahambre Road   36
The Way You Bounce Off a Pane of Glass   38

II
Or

Boots 43
Oysters on the Half Shell, and a Bottle of Red 45
Wanting Blue 47
Identity 49
The Predicament of Or 50
Cracks and Crevasses 61
Ending of Episode Three 67
Eclipse 69
An Attempt to Make a Promise 70
Declaration 72

III
The Quickened Diluvial Shore

Mouth 75
Magic Word 76
Lieveke in Antwerpen 77
Sometimes I Could 78
Mantra for Migrants 81
Language Poem 82
A Recognition 84
The Edited 86

Game of Watch the Migrant Dream, #1   88
Game of Watch the Migrant Dream, #2   91
All the Irish I Know   95
All the Hindi I Know   96
Bu' A A!   97
For Naan   99
Point of Convergence   102

IV
July Plum

The Unshakeable Man in Aldergrove   107
Waiting   110

I

The Way You Bounce Off a Pane of Glass

Beach Composition 1

Where is the room from which I heard
the clear slow dawn of parents?

Or was that the mutter of coconut fronds,
Rubbing themselves, scraping upside walls, sweeping the
       galvanized roof

Father's voice?
Rain on the roof

Humans sighed

Waves broke

Salt gnawed
the concrete foundation

Beach Composition II

Sea salt and ocean breeze
can pick apart flesh,
bones of this house, this childhood

only soft-bellied vultures
are spared

they play dead:

perch one-legged
atop metal marrow disintegrating
out of crumbling corner posts,

wrinkled eyes
half closed

Beach Composition III

Man-high moat of razor grass
keeps vandals, and me,
from trespass

Still, I saw what salt air does:

> wind, rain, vandals, time
> reduced steel reinforcements
> galvanized iron, concrete
>
> epidermis peeled
> crumbled
> like stale cake
> into cashmere-fine grounds
> of beach sand

No stubble of interior remains

Where is the refrigerator that shocked when we
        touched it?
Its metal skin peeled back
exposed gardens,
blossoms of red fungus.
Rust-petalled edges that could slice,
threatened us
with tetanus.

Even now, I reach for any refrigerator handle
and imagine it:
the phantom of electrocution
buzzing the length of a forearm

Portholes
are torn ragged from the roadside
where once there were beds, dining room, kitchen

    (salt slick
    oily grit
    dampened bedclothes
    sanded furniture,
    counter tops,
    linoleum and vinyl)

If this pen
could cut a path
I would walk it,
carry plaster and paint
outline each porthole,
frame a view

    of slow chop, lull of ocean,

    of horizon line,
    demarcation precise

    of equatorial sky,
    haze impregnable,

    of oil rigs for perspective, flames on top,
    a freighter here
    a frigate
    cloud

Still the air
tastes of blood, salt and rust,
the flavor of drinking water

Here is the cracked floor
of an outdoor bathroom stall

where a shower dripped water,
salty, singed the cornea

concrete walls wept,
spawned moss,

>   the crab cradled
>   in the bed
>   of slime-green moss

salt lichen florets flourished
on forearms, neck and legs

There was a camera, too—
in my hand and loaded—
but I could not bring myself to use it
for fear of what I would make:

>   realism
>   a theory
>   fiction
>   iconography
>
>   romancing the crumbling

The good thing about pen
and words:

    the plan to ensnare and remember

    is a true, a final,
    a most perfect forgetting

A Talent for Breathing

I remember there was that murky floor
In an unnamed ocean

It's a blur now
But I remember you spoke

Slow flatteries drooled,
Suffocated, insisted

And I heard—eyes closed, breath metered—
Someone who knew my name,
Exhibited me

Like a prima ballerina:
My talents, casual flamboyance,
Heel toe heel toe
All the way to the bottom

The talent for unassisted breathing
Under pressure, under water
Dancing me down to where catfish forage

To meet the one who knew my name
And called it

So slowly
Mistaken
For tenderly

Your bracing hands—
Bracing belly
To belly—
Wove a web,
Finer now
And tighter

And then?

Too late to untangle the strands
Those hands

Too late to see the distant surface
Of that thick and deep and murky sea

Glass and Lace Wrought Iron

Though you gave them the gold the bracelets the money
    the house
                a glass of ice-cold water

it's the sliding glass doors between me
and you
that protect me

from bandits
sworn to kill

Terrazzo patio, swing dressed-up, cushions in mango-yellow
vinyl, fence of bougainvilia oleander and philodendron,
dwarfing the house

cackle, hiss of kisskidee, banana quit and carib grackle,
palmettoes shushing all

I recall a horsewhip swaying,
hypnotic in a potted ornamental bamboo

❦

    "Carmen,"
(in the back grinding curry for crab)

    "what about snakes?"

From the kitchen comes garlic, curry paste and,

    "Snake? oh no, Lord! I fraid them too bad,
    dust out there this mornin self, didn't see none,
    them and me don't keep company, you does
    hardly see snake these days, I tell you."

❦

lushness and fear

checking behind and under cushions, I wonder:
where do her and my notion of 'hardly' intersect?

on the patio, needle-beaked black birds dive-bomb this
    trespasser

who keeps a lookout for bandits
they say will jump bougainvillia and chop down fern
in broad daylight to kill her

the hole in the hedge

overnight, you were legend

i saw you through the hole
in the hibiscus hedge

and knew ...

we had heard only half
the truth

in the hatchwork of leaves
twigs, bush, bush-bugs
i pull back, concealed,
and observe:

strolling down the hill, you make him
like he's never been made before

in the vicinity of you,
everything

everything is breath and breath is taken
away and
taken away

in Her evening swing
She reads the evening paper

She looks up and sees you
gossip about the town

She, from behind Her paper,

i in the hibiscus hedge,

see you clutch his elbow,
whisper in his ear
(though no one else can hear)

She calls out:
"Eh, look!
Is Billy.
Must be the new wife.
Is true what they say.
Come. I going to say hello."

She saunters down;
They introduce, they
introduce and introduce themselves

how you make them,
make everything,
beautiful

i still a caterpillar
in a hedge

Faith

my mother was Anglican
my father was a priest

they prayed hard together
and when spring came

they reaped the smoothest
stones you've ever seen.

Ceremonial

Fine
        White
                Line

Line white fine
Barely visible

Regard thy Father
Honor thy Mother

Buried in fine white linen

Exchanges

The radio in the car, barely audible.
What would you make of these miles of cane
this heat, these two people I ride with?

What would they think of you?

Her window's rolled up, but like a catcher's glove
she catches the hawker's eye and gestures:
"How much for your grapefruit?"

Pyramids of orange, portugal, grapefruit ripen, skins glisten
oily in dust,
in trembling roadside heat, haze of midday sun

From behind her makeshift counter the hawker sizes up
      the car, the driver, the madam;
she approaches...

"They have juice in them?"

... sweeps up the hem of her dress
and stoops at the window of this car.
"Yes man! They sweet.
I just cut one for the taxi driver over there. Look,
see how he enjoying it?"

Meanwhile, our driver comments:
"How you could ask her if they have juice?
You think she will tell you, 'no, they dry'?"

She doesn't hear him, busily exchanging
a bag of grapefruit for a grey ten dollar.
"Give me a bag of the portugals. Don't give me soft ones,
          eh?"

He grips the steering wheel,
stares at nothing in the distance.
"But you are something else! Of course she will include
          one or two soft ones.
She must get rid of them. Do you expect her to say,
          'Madam the orange ent sweet,
the grapefruit dry and the portugal soft,
but I begging you, buy them, na.
Look at car you driving, and I have child to mind'?"

She squeezes her purchases,
their inadequate bag of plastic.
"Hm! But these hard! You sure they have juice?"

In the rearview mirror, his eyes wait.
I consent to look and he locks on,
shakes his head.

But you learn, over time, not to meddle

※

She has leaned her seat back
and snores, that reassuring quiet rumble

A strand of hair falls across
her face

He takes his eyes off the road,
watches her

Removes a hand from the steering wheel

Rearranges the hair
with the lightest of fingers

Looks at her a little longer,
then back at the winding road.

With time, you learn not to worry or meddle:
They know each other. They have their ways.

❦

Wishing you were here, could see those hills ahead—
the ones we think of, here, as mountains.

Poui's Hero

Too stubbornly leaved;
unwanted lushness in the dry season;
damn thing, barren thing;
good for nothing but blocking the view;

> *But, of course! it's water-logged where it's planted!*

My father's argument
is not for sound landscaping
but a simple plea for a useless tree

Or is it something more
from this perennial opponent
of capital punishment?

> *Remember that season, years back when it flowered,*
> *and was magnificent?*

He produces the evidence:
yellowed photos, a painting—
crown and carpet in bas relief
knife-applied, waxy cadmium yellow

Once again, he facilitates a pardon,
tempers the landscape artist's wrath
and halts her executioner, the yardman's unwieldy ax

Now the damn thing stands,
none the wiser,
and surely won't flower next year

Hand-Held

Intending to contain
evidence of this
silver frame,
four by six

intending to capture
stone girl flower

everything is framed—everyone
that is, but you

stuffing leaks that spring
in bags of memory:

>   trickle of waterfall
>   erodes a valley

>   eucalyptus run amok
>   explosion embryonic

deep-rose rosella streaks
Katoomba's sky

bower birds shriek
stifled in a chemical stew

cockatoo-white cockatoos
I know from city zoos
and cool friends' closed-up apartments
ornament neighborhood foliage

Peter holds a glass by its stem,
in a salmon-coloured rocker
reclines in front of the fire

Ann and Abbas, arm in arm,
barefoot conquer the famously needle-strewn beaches
    of Bondi

Tracey by the front door yawning
and Tegan, Three Sisters behind her, squints the sun
    away

Everyone but you,
paralyzed on paper.

Manahambre Road

A handful of photographs shuffled,
a deck of cards fanned out.
I pick one ... an ace!

Princess Town to the left;
to the right San Fernando, Mon Repos;
Nadia in-between

I still hear her singing
"the sun slips behind the sea"

Checkerboard acres of arrowed cane
jagged horizon, Trinity Hills
range beyond range, alizarin crimson, navy blue

Roadside mango trees
> *their smell evoked*
> *in the corner store below,*
> *the Fiji imports*
> *plentiful in the cool spring air*

Nadia's smell ... gone gone gone we've been gone so long
> *I sniff the photo and smell*
> *Camphor balls from its box*

Eyes, gray. No! Light brown ... no ...
well, they were unusual anyway;
she's married now, two children, happy, they say.

Does she still compose poems
and songs for me,
still sing, "The sun
slips behind the sea"?

The Way You Bounce
Off a Pane of Glass

Mayaro Beach,
facing east

you talk of futures
etch your name
in vain with mangrove quill

you claim name-length portions of sand

coconut trees come all the way,
you say,
from the western shores
of Africa

today is today, you say,
just as the sea crawls up the sand,
washes your name away

moments used to be few
and far apart

now they line up
a stream of dots, islands,
vivid as sunlight reflected in glass

II
Or

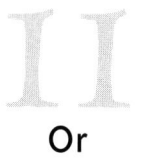

Boots

To celebrate my birthday,
bun high upon her head, she shot the kangaroo
mouthed wide that silent laugh, that Sheila.

Marsupial she dragged home
Marsupial she braised in brandy sauce
Sweet belt, what fire!

I had asked for kangaroo;
there were candles too.

Look at me, I begged.
She threw her head back and silent laughed

Elegant, lean, elbow on stone,
Glorious rage, such fire, frozen.

Trophies adorned the well-worn
mantelpiece
(how many books were imagined
before such eloquent stone?)

She pressed her kangaroo-leather boot
against this trembling chest;

as I was about to hold and touch and stroke
red red leather

she nudged precisely with her pointed toe
and I fell flat
on an author-trodden rug of sisal

She got to her feet,
she pressed that boot
against this chest
and said, Eat!

In kangaroo-leather
hunter home after the kill
glass slung in cheer

spill caught, right there, desire's shudder.

Oysters on the Half Shell, and a Bottle of Red

I admit that in the midst of quinces and cheeses I was
        thinking of cleavage

no wine spilled, no one to blame

Angusy oysters, yes, but no shells with scalloped fringes
on which her breasts (no sprig of parsley) might have come
        to rest

everything in due course and everything proper, she said

insisted she was not a flirt
and then dis-ordered with dessert:
poached quinces, cream cheese
quince juice the colour of rusty rose

(Jackson Pollack, master of the gesture,
could have yanked you/me
from your/my daze)

she knew this: *not everything,* she said, *but everything good*

and twirled muscat, swirled it around her tongue,
attended to carving slivers of quinces, shards of cheese

and me, I concocted a landscape for cleavage—
here, a fist full of Angusy nestled,
there, acreage of Sweet Necks, floral tight.

❧

Next morning:
a silver tray dressed in starched white linen
coffee glorious coffee
pomegranate
lychee in its ragged half nut
slices of starfruit
a newspaper
a danish

a solitary, pleasant breakfast,
spent measuring all
and everything good
against the facts and fictions of morning.
We parted last night;
shall we meet again, eat anew?

Wanting Blue

there's ink in this tongue

and if seeping could be sudden
the blue of it seeped suddenly
into my bones

erodable as limestone; more instant than eons
you vein through bone

and brittle, I dream in tones of Blue:

midnight in the Southern Hemisphere
more luminous than squid;
your hair so blue, it couldn't be anything but;
the taste of eucalypt in every liquid, every glass

there is no salt taste here
to remember you by
no net to crawl into
no Blundstones, no Newtown

this type of brief, this wanting—this thief in the night
        blue night—
slips,
if slipping could be sudden,
suddenly into the past

blue hair falling down your face
neckscent of eucalypt
skin pliant under T-shirt

I remember retreating (barely) when you turned and
        grabbed my waist

in all my remembrances, that laughing, that knowing,
certain as my name;
your smile smelled of mischief

moving towards you moving towards me
you closed your eyes

blue butterflies fell from your eyelids

Id

y					d

							ır eyes
are the color of the sky
that straddles the fiery North Sea

The Predicament of Or

The journey from Kamakura to Kyoto takes twelve days. If you travel for eleven, then stop with one day remaining, how can you admire the moon over the capital?

— NICHIREN, FEBRUARY 1280

1

It is remarkable
        worth remarking
how I am with you
      how you are with me.

11

In the springtime when rhododendrons—
when your blueshirt sparkles
and sunlight bounces—
>	off a trampoline

It is worth remembering—

the drenchings in milkweed-scented breezes,
being caught in that cherry-blossom petal storm,
sunscreen lotion creaming the outside pocket of
>	your pannier.
In the dry season, the raw heat of summer, that heavy
>	downpour—
>	>	that heavy downpour just when the pollen started to
>	>	thicken.

III

When does winter follow spring?

February, leaving Vancouver and cherry blossoms,
Arriving in New York,
Coat, gloves, scarf in hand.

IV

(In-between *is* a place)

Two juicers, two bottles of Vitamin C, two sets of
        memories—
one for there, another for here—
or is it: one for here, another for there
(*her mouth forms words, her eyes question, she smiles, I ...*) —
two bicycles, two helmets, two locks, two toothbrushes,
microwave ovens, postal codes, answering machines,
bedrooms, pairs of the same sandals, subscriptions to the
        same magazine,

"But what of the future?" I said. "Or ..."
and left it there
    (or was it here?)

V

May first, Five Finger Lakes, Upstate New York:

We were somewhere, passing over a bridge.
In the distance, too far away to hear,
a train appeared, disappeared, reappeared,
needle and thread, coursing through the fabric of trees.

>Canada Goose spotted:
>*Branta canadensis* on the lam.
>Is the Canada Goose Canadian?

>Blue jay crossing!
>Blue jay crossing!

Hoping for love, always hoping.

VI

June twelve, Highway 28A, Ashokan Reservoir, Olivetown:

We travelled down the middle of a country road.
Keeping your gaze straight ahead, you leaned over,
your eyes on the yellow line,
and kissed me—
the very hue of daffodils—

>Gopher!

>How much wood
>would a gopher
>go for
>if a gopher
>were to go for
>wood?

>Sparrow hawk! Sparrow hawk!
>Captures its prey on the ground!

Can you tell where we've been by the birds we've seen?

VII

It is remarkable
    worth remarking:
I used to call you "my sweet *Solanum Dulcamara*,"
my "*Lathyrus japonicus*,"
meaning: "something exciting"

VIII

Now two months have passed
since we last kissed. Remember?
8:30 pm: I kissed your lips,
I am about to / your hand is ...
8:39 pm: Stop! Look! Across the water,
behind a stand of trees,
the sun slips.
Take a picture!
And another!
8: 49 pm: A persimmon
slips ...
8:50 pm: Jagged thread of fire
turns the lake, 8:56 pm, to champagne

The sky—not you, not I—ignited,
9:01 pm.

IX

It is worth asking:
Home, are you coming home? When
are you coming home?

Then let us talk of home:
Does one *come* home
or
Does one *go* home?

> *If you stop with one day remaining,*
> *how can you admire the moon?*

x

Solanum dulcamara, violet and mustard:
Fluorescent red
Bitter succulence
Somnambulism teasing sedation

In the heat of summer, when *Solanum dulcamara* sweeps
city sidewalks, cracks pavement, foot-stools every post,
street corners and fields ablaze,
berries burst juices and whisper your name.
In the heat of summer,
when *Solanum dulcamara* creeps and blows
your scent, air, oxygen itself,
I dream of you, only you,
and touch myself.

    My sweet *Solanum dulcamara, Lathyrus japonicus*

XI

Every day is the eleventh day.

XII

And the moon? My love, remember this:
the evening moon rises
everywhere.

Cracks and Crevasses

I

if you can make it there
you can make it . . .

    you know how the story goes

but I did not sleep with the city at night;
it is you I miss now I'm gone

I learned about glaciers

by falling into
exploring
the crevice of you

there is a snow coming:
town country city sea-shore look the same
Canada Geese are everywhere

in the heart, in the heat
of night, what is it I know and you don't?

your flight of smile, your weathered
punches

there is a snow coming
and I must leave

leave you before the chill

11

F26 window-seat over
Verano Brooklyn Manhattan
Empire State Twin Towers Chrysler
stretching this high up—taxi ruckus
cloistered breath of a subterranean train

mercilessly clear
Long Island Fire Island Shelter Island
Jones Beach right there right there, that very parking lot

high above patchwork plains
Manitoba then Saskatchewan then Alberta
white-lipped salt lakes and land so parched and caked
one wonders why that clump of houses

who and why that road, that field

from a cloudless sky you emerge into the snow below;
a security checkpoint separated us not three hours ago:
kisses blowing blowing blown
as we move away, one from the other
waving good-bye

or was that, "come back,
don't go don't go"

Calgary Kananaskis the Rockies below
Victoria Banff Louise
bow rivers in the valleys

blurring fogging

glacier matterhorn arete
the scent of your side of the bed
hanging valley
body of water tarn
or was that light
was that shadow
like your business-voice chatter
wafting in from another room

that first time

III

where the glacier has receded
the land is scorched—
glacial burn

the heart that is between
goodbye and hello-you-over-there
is brackish
fore and aft colliding

in city, town and country, sea-shore,
a brackish heart is fickle

IV

this I know, this you know

> *Travel on glacial ice is*
> *dangerous*

this by now
we ought to know

> *variation in flow rates*
> *between different parts of a glacier*
> *causes stresses forms cracks forms crevasses*

> *chasmal fissures conceal*
> *bridges of snow*

> *sometimes*
> *thick enough*
> *to hold a body*

> *and sometimes not.*

Ending of Episode Three (also known as "Gate C")

As she was turning again towards the gate I scraped breath
for a lips-to-fingers kiss

that was probably too hesitant, wet with intent
weighted with wonderings and promises to fly

In any case she'd already turned, resigned

The shine of our raincoat sculpted her back
(first thing in the morning, I have come to know,
she smells of roses)

At Gate C
I watched her merge

wearing sunglasses (removed earlier
to facilitate the closer hug, the tighter kiss)
my kissing hand fisted
in the pocket of this
fleece jacket

one step forward one step more
one more
and

she was gone

through the open mouth
sharp little teeth
of Gate C

Eclipse

The day of your arrival
is tagged, like a present—
your name engraved upon it.

Alter the plan, if you must.
But think: what will come of that day?
No one else can open it.

An Attempt to Make a Promise

A butch's worth:
    word in the hand
    telescoped

The navigator's bone
    not a sliver
    not a trace
    of home

Stings and allegories,
    bee pollen by spoonfuls—
golden antidote to stings—and

How many birds are there in a hand these days,
if these days there are none in the bush?

From her bathwater, a saucer
    of tight-fisted rose buds,
little teeth bloodied and gums

A butch's word
    in the hand:
wet concrete forming

beads. A souvenir
necklace—

her weight is her words in
    gold

that stunt your growth
with their concrete weight

From around my neck
I removed the frame
of Cathedral Gold

Declaration

though she's alone
no stone
in hunger
will she suck

nor dirt
in cracks
will she mistake
for fragrant snacks

she has learned
she must pick
she dares to choose

    &

sated, there's no need
to pile her plate
eye-high
                    with bones

III

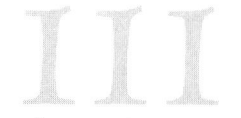

The Quickened Diluvial Shore

Mouth

fat fish

tread

ing
water

flip
pin
f/s/lap
pin

silversilver
sil

ver
gainst

thequickened
gainstthequickened

                                                    dilu vial shor e

Magic Word

upon forecurl of tongue
the word "please"
shapeshifted

edible
ricepaper
perfumed gossamer shrivelling

pressed through teeth
a too-ripe fruit
exploding

trombone
sky to sea
to sky and back

metal against metal
brake into Bergen
the F train's precarious cornering

Lieveke in Antwerpen

bedside table, glassful of chatter
eau de source petillante
lieverd lieverd lieverd
palm to knuckle to finger

hand that taxes the heart

wrist to kiss to severe, slow curl of gesture
petulant water
lieverd lieverd lieverd
lunatic lovesick roaming the Grote Markt

gossips the bruisend bronwater

Sometimes I Could

When I was too young
for her to have known
that I would travel far from home
my Mother cried, in vain:
>"You have no respect for   family
>One day you'll wish you had   family
>One day you'll hold your head and bawl: "family"

Each day for a decade
I wondered if
how
that one day, that family,
that particular ...

how?

Then the other
day—and not just another
day, another lover,
though the day rolls in, at first, like any other
lover—a day like a wave

a lover like a final straw
splayed thin, thinned out and disappeared up-shore

That particular day I wished,
That day my head,
That bawl

❦

Family
I left behind
parade themselves,
details fresh in my mind:
mother father siblings uncles aunts
cousins, nephews, nieces.
Some I know only through photographs

Family
I left behind,
family I searched for

in every person who shares this color of skin
in each new "back home" novel,
each poem postcard conversation film

in everyone who mutters
"I know exactly what you mean …"

    And I hold this respect, this wish
    this head,
    this bawl.

Mantra for Migrants

Always becoming, will never be
Always arriving, must never land

Between back home and home unfathomable, is me—
By definition: immigrant

I'll always be oh glorious
Glorious unchangeable

In truth, I am in flux
Immigrant I will forever be
Migrant oh yes, oh migrant me

Migrant immutable amazing unchangeable

Always becoming, will never be
Always arriving, must never land

I pledge citizenship, unerring
Loyalty, to this State of Migrancy

Language Poem

```
It
      is
that         a
      I            crime
to           should
      use          have
to           your
      tell         language
I            you
      feel        how
have         that
      taken       you
             mine
                   from
me
```

something bruised   brews inside   (no language to describe)   but when I find   my voice   I know I must take care …

                                        not
                                to
                        scream   loudly
                so   in
                        your   that
                direction   I
                        do   what
                to   you
        you   have
                done
        to

                                        me

A Recognition

"You're Trinidadian!"
I blurt out proudly, smugly,
accusation not, of course, intended.
"I recognize the accent!"

Mine suddenly dips deep, curves like a kite,
thickens like sugar browning in oil for stew.

>Our paths would likely not have crossed
>back there
>so why is it
>I throw myself upon her over here?

Before I have time to ask
>"So where you come from?"
>"What's your name?"
>"Who's your mother, where's your father?"

she has turned,
but I hear her say, "I am Canadian,"
the reply dropped flat,
mercilessly terse

These are things I know:
anonymity, autonomy
freedom to self-define
to forget
to come out
to escape

sometimes there is (something I understand)
no room to negotiate

The Edited

hap-pens to deleted
words? th speed at which fall?

I venture most not float
like sakura petals but

drop hard ndfast biting met
al clink of iron key goug

ing sidewalks & other port
ions of earth, they lurk

idle n West End alleys
gather round wheels

postponed shopping trolleys may
be in th darkened parts of

city parks well from
eyes of stone nd clay nd oth

er places good citizens ought
to (but don't)

at last reconnoiter a
word deemed redundant was spotted

not 5ifty meters from nd
advancing tward an alpine

meadow deemed endangered such
errant missiles booby

traps mines deletion is rare
ly convincingly abslute

Game of Watch the Migrant Dream, #1

PROLOGUE:
Destination

At your service   masterful dreamer   (in need of a job)
doesn't do just anything   for a pittance
but your pleasure primary of course
she dreams   as migrants often do
(yes, some will charge you less   but not all dreams
and wanderers are created …)

You may, as you will,
take notes
pictures

PERFORMANCE:
The Recurring Dream

Plane of the recurring dream—itinerants aboard!

The airplane of the recurring dream travels
an asphalt highway
built on stilts, a flyway of solid ground

The acceleration of the recurring dream
is as fast as the speed of the plane:
Nose preceding, body angled, rising ...

Back wheels remain rivetted
to solid ground.

In the temple of the recurring dream, travel is horizontal—
lift-off and arrival, like belief, are suspended.

Passengers become occupants,
drifters from seat to seat,
their motion unceasing—
seat-belts buckled, unbuckled, buckled—
mesmerized window-seat watchers
while landmarks blur: tree, stone, concrete

In the plane of dreams
lift-off is unexpected
there's no pilot, no flight crew

Destination:
necessarily unattended
comfortably unattained

Game of Watch the Migrant Dream, #2

PROLOGUE

Abyss fissure chasm canyon crevasse crack
On one side note-takers abundant
pencil they   notepad in hand
On the other side, migrant she   rope-ladder,
intention to cross, in tow

One side bugle calls
Signal start   of this performance

PERFORMANCE:
Another Recurring Dream
I

Gathered up rope-ladder   Migrant swings swing
swing swing swing
Momentum achieved (to be sure)
She flings   F   L   I   N G
Rope hits one side, note-takers roar

oh god rope slipping   slippery slope

Crowd coaxes migrant's rope
note-takers squeal but rope a metre short
pulled back back and slips slowly off
off by its own weight, imagine!

Note-takers take notes   too busy, of course
and pictures (to be sure)
busy busy they
but migrant she   proud migrant dreaming   proud she
Takes rope-hauling   like a course
retrieves hope dangling (par for the course)
Abyss fissure chasm canyon crevasse crack

11

Once re-gathered rope ladder bugle calls
swing swing swing swing swing swingswung
Doing the migrant fling (momentum, to be sure!)
      F   L   I   N G
Rope (at least this) arrives one side, bigger uproar
    But   and   but   rose lips

        Crowd analysis:
migrant's materials methods nature nurture, to be sure!
Dream a metre short, damn oh dear,
(its very own weight length—imagine!) lips lowly off

Note-takers watch   migrant hauling   hope
    busy busy busy no takers watch

She migrant this   migrant flinging
    dream   other side dreaming
Inch by inch   hours of haul   hope as long as deep as
Abyss fissure chasm canyon crevasse crack

III

renewed   undeterred   rope-ladder   swing
swings   wingswungswungswungswingswing
swung Momentum achieved, whose for sure?
FL   I   N G falls
far from one side different crowd bigger furor
some uh uhs no buts no ands no oars
crowd hoaxes   rope squeals a metre short
so much for hauling weight (imagine that its
own its weight) lips lowly slips solely it's another
migrant falling another migrant mauling for sure

All The Irish I Know

Oh Sullivan! Oh Keefe! Oh Sharkey!
Mc Namee Siobhan Mcguire.
Naill Erin banshee begorrah?
Elish ni gwivnamacort,
Kavanagh!

Healy Mcliamurphy.
Dermot durcan, Healy!
Oh Sullivan, Oh Keefe, Oh Sharkey!
Leprechaun begorrah!

All The Hindi I Know

Acha
Chalo
Aap ke naam kya hai?
Bayti bayta,
Meera naam Shani hai.

Dhadi Dhada,
Nahi
Hai

Bu' A A!

Hardi aloo: Sita Gita Meethai!
Paymee dhal koorma?
Aloo pone tabanka!
Baigan peewah,
Jhunjut mamaguy.

Jheera jhundi,
"Gulab jamon chokha,"
Pooja
Busup-shirt joovay.
Googlie jhunjhut calalloo,
Pholourie- Pandit Panday!

Mauby: sagaboy pone pelau,
Sorrell shadow-benny pastel.
Doodoose
La jablesse jagabat?
Careete!
Corailee parang.

Moko jumbie
Pone bara,
Agoutie chip-chip ackra!

For Naan

The alarm clock radio blurts out: CBC-Vancouver,
Fluorescent red glow pries me awake
To hear a letter from two flight attendants from New West

On Holiday!

Pawing the foothills of the Nepalese Himalayas
Enamored of the primitive lives
Of beautiful smiles, white teeth
Of brass bells tinkling tinkling
On beasts of burden as they trek over
This pass, that summit—
How they wished to remain as long as they could
Before returning
To civilization;
If you're planning a trip,
Keep in mind it costs only ten rupees,
Or thirty cents, per night for a bed. What a deal!

They brought back trophies of authentic Kulu Valley topi.

Images I have hoarded jealously
From *National Geographic*
Span panoramic across my mind.
But how it irks me to know the color of the hills
Before the snow blues everything,
To know of pebbly faces creased like the hills,
To know of Naan's girlhood clothing swirling
Dusty red, dandelion, saffron
With sequins iridescent and beads of glass,
To know of yaks, yak butter, remote mountain culture,
To know of all these,
From travelogues, adventure journals and PBS-TV.

How it berserks me
That I have exoticized
My great-grandmother's land,
That someone else relentlessly
Tames conquers colonizes gazes objectifies leaves pawmarks
Where I can only dream of an embrace

If I were to do the White thing and pilgrimage there
Would my cousins, I wonder, gladly see Naan in me?
And I, Naan in them?
Do *I* dare wear a topi?
It's been so long that I, with my mineable traces
Of authentic Nepalese,

Surely *I* appropriate if *I* dare to wear
A topi from the Kulu Valley.

Let me suggest something:
When my presence in this land irks you
When your eyes curse me
Brown as I am
Other as I am
Ancestor of the pebbly face,
Remember how you love to climb all over
My great-grandmother's mountains, this pass, that summit
Primitive lives beautiful smiles white teeth
Brass bells tinkling tinkling, beasts of burden trek

Remember how you are charmed by my Naan's quaint ways
(as long as she stays in her place)
And remember how you love to photograph all of this
In another land.

Point of Convergence

union of back home
way back then, and home

where *I* depend neither
on memory nor desire
where *I* am neither
mendhi, baigan, steelpan

nor mindless of these

it's a seamless concoction,
like mulligatawny: cooks long and slow,
neither jheera, cardamom, hurdi
nor clove
stand alone

it's hybridity,
as in: "offspring of tame sow and wild boar,
child of freeman and slave"*

some new stew
or callaloo

spotted variegated deformed crude
new

Calcottawarima
persimango-orangegrapepear
Vancouverlaromainottawa
pommeracappleplummecythere

where neither Nepalese great-grandmother
nor mother, lover, government
define *I*

nor am
I
mindless of these

* (Oxford English Dictionary, seventh edition)

IV

July Plum

The Unshakeable Man in Aldergrove

In Aldergrove a man has a house on the verge
of a view: mountain ranges, shades of blue
craggy peaks flecked with summer snow. In winter
those mountains—he points—are dark blue.
Mount Baker's perennial dollop of icing

changes its colour on evenings,
chameleon to the variables, temperate sky.
I can describe it all
say that everything here is *like* something else
but today the sky is blue, sky-blue,

flowers bloom, clouds are shaped,
twin engines hum—it's a clear day—eagles eye
tiny dogs they have mistaken for rabbits.
The man in Aldergrove has ambition.
I want to be like those … over there (he points) …
      mountains.

His wife, she says friends are here
and so the cost of lunch is insignificant
and the day—the sky is blue, sky-blue—is magnificent,
the breeze silk, the silk breeze embracing, breathing
        silk air ...
its amazing how things just fit together.

The man with the house on the verge
of two-and-a-half acres in Aldergrove,
pulls up dandelions and mows his lawn before dinner.
During dinner he watches one neighbour's verdant field:
tree-boundaried, dots of silos and barns, flecks of cattle.

There is a hayfield in front of my house, he says,
sloping, silent—it's a hot hot summery day—and
        sprawling,
there is a hayfield between me and my mountains.
But it's not my hayfield, he says, smiling apologetically,
someone else has to cut it.

After dinner the man on the verge
turns up the Gypsy Kings on his tapedeck.
His dogs howl at evening phantoms
and he, relaxed and confident, dances, *chachachacha*,
with his twirling wife, laughing.

Watching the ranges and ranges of mountains
sundown golds, twilight orange, he reflects:
he wishes his life were unshakeable …
he gestures, open palm, as if to say, *da-da-da-dum* …
unshakeable as a mountain.

Waiting

I

They say you're coming,
You'll be here before the fraying of a year—
This time, certain as consequence,
As sea-side dawn and July plum

The boys, the girls
The brass band and the architect
The editor, critic
Home-maker, sushi chef
They're all saying
(Their magnolia assurance infectious)
You're definitely ... it's confirmed ... you're coming

11

I fear it's been said before.
Will I wait again, in vain?
But I bet you knew—
In the past, you would have come and I would have clung
    to my branch
Concerned about all I was lacking
A fruit green enough to chill thought, sour enough to
    shrivel hope

But this time they're shouting it through
The throats of their universe-connected umbilicus

You'll be arriving any day soon, so they're polishing up,
Building towers and treasures and cities and futures
With faxes, pamphlets, plans, determinations

Drum-tight hearts tremble the wait away
They dance, banners above them,
The wind and sun, the auspices of faith,
Rainbow crests bobbing in the sea, they know you're finally
    coming
Light impressing a corner, rounding a corner, a rudder, an
    anchor, the knowing
Sea breeze, moon, the length of a day waiting

In a corner, an idea writes a song
The ikebana ladies fillet flowers
The playwright and the conductor
Design poisons and medicines, charms for a storm
There is a group in the basement weaving a banner
With reeds peeled from the muscles of their hearts
A lady on a ladder costumes walls
While someone makes a ruckus with a microphone

In a corridor, in a tower, the choir braids words
Ssomeone uncovers a voice, a color, a note

They polish, they polish
They polish and they polish

Now I feel in my navel the certainty, the pull
Ocean's early tides tossing gifts to the dawn

And this time, this time I'll be a
Star, the sand, night, a full moon
Waiting

III

I've stocked up the refrigerator
There's ice in the icebox
Food in the pot on the stove
I swept
Polished mirrors and made the bed

I'm all dressed up, ready and waiting

Let me know when your plane gets in—
I'll be there, my car tank is full
The tires are pumped, I'm ready to roll

I'm so overwhelmed I fear I'll be unable to talk
So I'll be bringing
The boys and the girls
The brass band and the architect
The editor
The man at the corner store
The hairdresser, the movie buff
The sushi chef and the bookseller

This time, I know you're coming
Only because, this time,
I'm ready, willing, waiting.

Acknowledgements

"Beach Composition I" is for Ramesh
"Beach Composition II" is for Indrani
"Beach Composition III" is for Vahli
"Glass Lace and Wrought Iron" is for Kavir
"Exchanges" is for Vanita
"Poui's Hero" is for Arini
"Bu A'A" is for Stephan
"The Way You Bounce Off a Pane of Glass" is for Sitara
"Waiting" is for Daisaku Ikeda
"The Unshakeable Man in Aldergrove" was written with thanks to Leaigh Nishibata, Anthony Nishibata, Ben and Hidemi Nishibata, Marilyn Bodnarchuck and Taijun Kawamoto for contributing some of the lines and images in this poem.

I would like to thank Kate Braid, Dionne Brand, Cathy Stonehouse and Shauna Paull for their generous encouragement. Acknowledgement is due also to Michelle Benjamin, Emiko Morita and Val Speidel at Raincoast Books and the Polestar Imprint. Finally, I extend heartfelt gratitude to my editor Lynn Henry, and to Maria Massie of Witherspoon Associates.

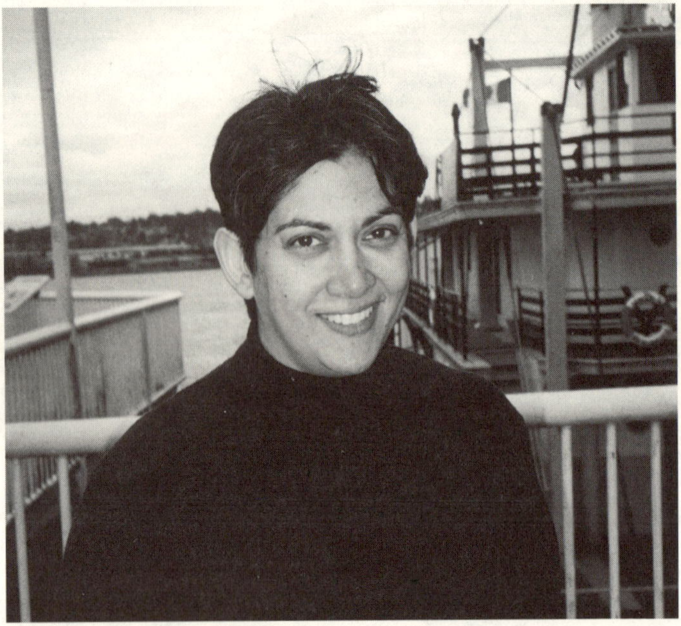

About the Author

SHANI MOOTOO was born in Ireland and grew up in Trinidad. She is the author of a book of short stories, *Out on Main Street* (Press Gang), and a novel, *Cereus Blooms at Night* (McClelland and Stewart), which was shortlisted for the Chapters First Novel Award and the Giller Prize. Her poetry has been anthologized in *The Very Inside*, *The Skin on our Tongue*, *Heat #12* and *West Coast Line*. In addition to being a writer, Shani is a video-maker and visual artist whose paintings and photo-based work are exhibited internationally. She lives in Vancouver, British Columbia.

Bright Lights *from* Polestar Book Publishers

Polestar takes pride in creating books that enrich our understanding of the world, and in introducing superb writers to discriminating readers.

POETRY

Blue • by George Elliott Clarke
Blue is black, profane, surly, damning, and unrelenting in its brilliance. George Elliott Clarke has written urgent and necessary poems about the experience of being black in North America.
1-55192-414-5 $18.95 CAN/$13.95 USA

FICTION

What's Left Us • by Aislinn Hunter
Six stories and a novella by a prodigiously talented new writer. "Aislinn Hunter is a gifted writer with a fresh energetic voice and a sharp eye for the detail that draws you irresistibly into the intimacies of her story."
—Jack Hodgins
1-55192-412-9 $21.95 CAN/$15.95 USA

Stubborn Bones • by Karen Smythe
"Karen Smythe brings to her fiction a combination of sharp intelligence and delicate sensibility. With a few deft strokes she manages, in these understated stories, to create a mood—lyrical and elegaic—that haunts the reader long after the book is finished." —Joan Givner
1-55192-364-5 $21.95 CAN/$15.95 USA

Daughters are Forever • by Lee Maracle
Maracle's new novel reinforces her status as one of the most important First Nations writers. A moving story about First Nations people in the modern world and the importance of courage, truth and reconciliation.
1-55192-410-2 $21.95 CAN/$15.95 USA

diss/ed banded nation • by David Nandi Odhiambo
"Thoroughly convincing in its evocation of young, rebellious, impoverished urban lives ... an immersion into a simmering stew of racial and cultural identities…" —*The Globe and Mail*
1-896095-26-7 $16.95 CAN/$13.95 USA

Pool-Hopping and Other Stories • by Anne Fleming
Shortlisted for the Governor-General's Award, the Ethel Wilson Fiction Prize and the Danuta Gleed Award. "Fleming's evenhanded, sharp-eyed and often hilarious narratives traverse the frenzied chaos of urban life with ease and precision." —*The Georgia Straight*
1-896095-18-6 $16.95 CAN/$13.95 USA